ENLIGHTENMENT
FOR
BEGINNERS

Also by Chuck Hillig

The Magic King
The Way IT Is
Seeds for the Soul
Looking for God

ENLIGHTENMENT FOR BEGINNERS

Discovering the Dance of the Divine

Chuck Hillig

Illustrated by
Colleen McDougal Mills

SENTIENT PUBLICATIONS

First Sentient Publications edition 2006

Copyright © 2006 by Chuck Hillig

Originally published as *What Are You Doing in My Universe?* © 1977,
1979 Black Dot Publications

Cover design by Kim Johansen
Book design by Timm Bryson

Library of Congress Cataloging-in-Publication Data

Hillig, Chuck.
  [What are you doing in my universe]
  Enlightenment for beginners : discovering the dance of the divine /
written by Chuck Hillig ; illustrated by Colleen McDougal Mills.
    p. cm.
  Originally published: What are you doing in my universe. San
Bernardino, Calif. : Borgo Press, 1983.
  ISBN 1-59181-040-X
  1. Philosophical anthropology–Miscellanea. I. Title.

BD450.H56 2006
128.02'07–dc22

2005037664
Printed in the United States of America
10 9 8 7 6 5 4 3 2 1

SENTIENT PUBLICATIONS, LLC
1113 Spruce Street
Boulder, CO 80302
www.sentientpublications.com

ATTENTION

THIS BOOK IS OFFICIAL CLUE # 4325

This is really a book about YOU.

It's a little story about who you *really* are and how (and why) you became what you are pretending to be.

This book is not meant to instruct you or to give you any new information. It's just here to remind you about something that you keep forgetting about yourself.

Something rather ASTONISHING!

But don't worry. If you don't get it this time either, you'll just remind yourself about it again... *later on!*

If I am I
because you are you,

and if you are you
because I am I,

then I am not I
and you are not you.

—Old Hasidic Saying

REALITY
A POINT OF DEPARTURE

If you're a young kid, you might just want to skip this first section completely and get directly into the fun part of the book itself. That's OK. This introduction has actually been written for the bigger people who might be needing some more background in preparation for their "journey."

Anyway (if you're still reading this), I don't want you to *believe* anything that's in this book. (And, yes, I really do mean that.) I especially don't want you to trade in your beliefs for what you think are my beliefs. I'm also not looking for your agreement about anything, and I'm certainly not interested in being *right*. Since none of these things are really provable anyway (at least, not in the usual sense), I only want you to consider them as possibilities!

OK, so here's the Big Question: Do you really know the difference between what is real and what isn't real? Yes, I know that you think you do, but the actual truth about it may really not be that simple.

So, this little book is here to show you how (and why) you've been fooling yourself into mistaking the appearance of reality for Reality itself.

Why is this so important? Well, since you've gotten a bit confused about what's really *real* out there, you've forgotten something about yourself that's absolutely, well, INCREDIBLE!

In fact, it's so easy to forget this special "something" that, believe it or not, you've actually created a lot of different ways to help you to remember it again! Who knows? Maybe this little book will turn out to be one of many thousands of clues that you've secretly arranged for yourself.

So, here's a quick test to take when you're finished reading: if a deep part of your heart begins to resonate with what's being implied here, then your latest reminder to yourself has been successful.

Anyway, let's start with where you're at right now. At the bottom line, you probably consider that the universe is really made up of only two basic things: first, of course, there's you, and then there's everything else that's not you. Or, to put it another way, what-you-say-you-ARE is very different from what-you-say-you-are-NOT.

In fact, ever since you were an infant, you've been assuming that the common boundary between these two opposing realms (the I and the not-I) was determined by the physical outline of your own body.

Pretty simple, right?

Although you'll get a lot of cultural support for this separatist point of view, please remember that much of man's history has been painfully shaped by the conflicts that this belief has created.

Even our western religions openly assert that there's a fundamental separation that exists between man and God. You know the old story: because we're all so sinful, they say, we have to struggle hard on this earth in the hopes of, someday, being united with God in heaven. It's a fascinating story, and it certainly has created a lot of melodrama.

But now I'd like you to consider another story. You see, this dualistic model of the universe can be simplified even one step further. Instead of the two things that you had before (*you* and *everything else*), what would happen if you began to consider the universe as just being YOU?

In other words, in spite of what appears to be to the contrary, YOU may actually be (for lack of a better term) what IS.

That's right! You = the Universe! Yes, absolutely A L L of It! *The whole enchilada!*

Now, when you begin looking at yourself that way, then any feelings of separation automatically disappear! Why? Because, if there's nothing that's NOT you, then there's nothing that you can ever be truly separated from! And, for that matter, there would be no one really "there" to be doing the "separating" anyway! Everything (and "everybody") would be, quintessentially, only ONE. Period!

Now, if you're still with me on this, let's walk down this path a little further.

When this imaginary line dissolves between what-you-say-you-ARE, and what-you-say-you-are-NOT, then both of these positions are discovered to be only points of view. In a cosmic instant, any perceived separation between the "you" and the "not-you" is suddenly recognized for being what it truly is: just an *illusion!*

Yes, I totally agree with you. The appearance of the world-as-real is very convincing, extremely melodramatic, and utterly fascinating. But, just like the mirage of a lake in the desert, its essence may only be illusory!

Still aboard? Good! Then let's take another step.

If all separation between you and everything else is, in fact, an illusion, then the so-called "reality" that you experience seems to take on some of the characteristics of a film that's being projected on a movie screen.

For example, when you watch an exciting movie, it's very easy to get pulled into the emotional drama that's unfolding on the screen. But, as you start identifying yourself with the characters and getting swept up into the storyline, *what happens to the screen?*

Well, it's still there, of course, but you're just not consciously aware of it anymore. The superimposed movie has, seemingly, "divided" the unbroken screen into moving characters and backgrounds that are all working together to hold your attention by evoking some kind of emotional response. But here's the point: Without the presence of the underlying screen to reflect the light vibrations that are being projected, nothing ever really happens!

So, in truth, couldn't we rightfully say here that the screen itself is the *only* fundamental reality?

Here's where we're going with this: if separation is truly illusory, then, perhaps, a very similar phenomenon could also be happening for you, too.

Now, please consider the following only as a possibility. Maybe, just maybe, there's a kind of illusory *you* who seems to be appearing in an on-going film that's called *My Life*. You're the *star* of this cosmic drama, of course, and, obviously, you also have a rather large *supporting cast* (complete with lots of heroes and villains) who, periodically, enter and exit your *stage* on cue.

But there's a catch: In order to be able to interact dramatically with these so-called "others," you have to first experience yourself as a disconnected ego. *In short, you have to pretend to be playing out a role in this drama as a separate individual. In other words, you have to be a "person!"*

However, just like in the movie, the actual reality that underlies your role in the world might also be like a kind of unbroken and seamless screen, too. In truth, this very screen that is supporting the dramatization of your individual movie role may actually be, deep down, WHO you really are! It may, in fact, be your very own true nature!

This is not a new idea, of course. In fact, historically, this screen has been given many different names, e.g., Consciousness, Tao, the Self, the Brahman, Spirit, Oneness.

In fact, the oldest eastern religions have long recognized this Great Illusion as *lila*—the divine dance. By completely giving up his attachment to the role that he is playing in his life, the seeker becomes awakened to the pure consciousness that he really always was all along. In a sense, he *becomes* the screen itself by discovering that he already *is* who he has been looking for!

To produce this radical awakening, however, most eastern religions initially follow the traditional path of surrendering to some deity or guru. Because of this, eastern religions may often appear to be as dualistic as western religions.

This path of surrender attracts many spiritual seekers,

from both east and west, because such an approach provides them with specific guidelines for their devotion. These include traditional dogmas, ritualized ceremonies, and the promise of a heavenly reward.

But, there's a big paradox here: the seeker's very efforts to experience enlightenment only reinforces, once again, this same persistent illusion that he is, fundamentally, separated from the very goal that he is seeking. When that happens, it just triggers still more struggling, which, once again, only reinforces yet a further experience of separation.

And on and on and on.

It has been said that the greatest obstacle to enlightenment is getting past your belief that you are not already enlightened!

So, what can you do?

The problem, of course, is that you can't easily talk about any of this. Since words are dualistic, you can quickly get caught up in a lot of paradoxical feedback loops. After all, says Alan Watts, a fingertip can't really point at itself!

Well, maybe it can. But first you need to point it at a mirror! The secret, though, lies in recognizing the image in the mirror (the world that you see) for being what it truly is—just a perfect reflection of who you are. In that profound realization, you open your heart to loving whatever shows up for you in the world as your very own Self! Your ground-of-being becomes LOVE loving ITSELF!

This same universal Truth (often called the perennial philosophy) has been found in the spiritual literature of all of the great cultures around the world and across the ages.

But this time, however, your gentle reminder to yourself is really very simple. In fact, the main text contains just a little over 2,000 words, and you can easily go through it in under 30 minutes. I suggest that you first read the book several times yourself, and then share it with your friends. Please remember, though, that it's only one of many reminders that you've placed along your path. As you become more open to noticing them, they'll start to show up for you as grace.

So, once again, please don't take my word about any of this. As I said earlier, this is not about believing something new. Your true nature can *only* be discovered experientially, so look within your heart and see for yourSelf!

Above all, let go of your ego's desire to want to logically figure it all out. Your rational mind will never be able to become enlightened. Instead, simply trust in the willingness of your heart to being reminded again about something that it has known all along.

You've forgotten about this for a while. But right now, if you're ready, maybe you'll allow yourself to . . .

REMEMBER

Do you know **who** you are?

I mean,

do you

really

k n o w

?

Oh, I don't mean your *name*.

That's not *who* you are.

That's what you are *called*.

OK, then, you say,

if I'm NOT my *name*, then...

WHO AM I?

WHO am I?

Who **AM** I?

Who am **I**?

Am I my body?

Am I my  thoughts?

Am I my feelings?

do

DO

DO   do

Am I... what I **DO?**

DO   **do**

do

And who are YOU,
and what are YOU
doing in
MY universe?

Well, since I really don't *seem*
to know *who* I am—

(and, since I have to
begin *somewhere*)

let's just say that
I'm this **BLACK DOT.**

OK, then, if I AM
this **BLACK DOT,**

then I have shape,
I have **color**,
and I have **S I Z E** .

Well, then, if what I **AM**
looks like THIS,

●

then what I am **NOT**
has to look like THIS!

●

Now, wait a minute!

They both look like the same thing!
Let's do that one again—

S   L   O   W   L   Y   !

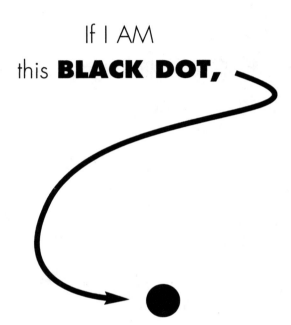

If I AM
this **BLACK DOT,**

then what I am NOT is this

WHITE SPACE

around   me.

(Hmmm, that's interesting.
They sure look like the same thing!)

Well, now I'm getting confused!

Am I a **BLACK DOT** on
a **WHITE SPACE**,

O R

am I a **WHITE SPACE**
with a **BLACK DOT?**

 ?

Oh, this is ridiculous!

Of course I'm the
BLACK DOT!

!

See? This is **ME!**

●

And so *this*

is what is NOT **ME!**

●

(Hmmmmm. Now why do
they still look the SAME?)

When I show ME
and when I show
what is not ME,

the pictures look exactly **alike!**

What's going on here?

 ?

Does what I **AM**
depend on
what I am **NOT?**

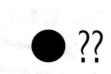

Well, let's find out.

If I'm this **BLACK DOT,**

and I take away the
WHITE SPACE around me,
then what happens to
the **BLACK DOT?**

What happens to **ME?**

Hmmmmm...

So If I take away what is not **ME**,
                (the **WHITE SPACE**)

then all that's left...
                is **ME!**

Hey! Look at **that!**
If I'm all-there-IS, then I'm

EVERYTHING

and I'm

EVERYWHERE!

WOW!

This is pretty neat! If I want to *GO* someplace, I won't even have to move because I'm already

THERE!

But wait a minute now!

How can I really *GO* anyplace?

I mean, if I'm all-there-is,
then there's no other "place"
that I can really, well, *GO!*

Hey, I think that being

EVERYThING

E V E R Y W H E R E

is going to get really **boring**
after a while! Let's go back
to the way it was, OK?

WHEW!

●

OK, that seems a little more
interesting than all of that BLACK!

Well, me being

EVERYTHING

E V E R Y W H E R E

was pretty boring because
there was nothing to "DO"

(and, for that matter, nobody "ELSE"
to be doing it with anyway!)

So now what do I do?

I know!
Let's try it the other way.

What if I take away
the thing that IS **ME?**

Let's see what happens when
I take *away* the black dot.

HEY!

I like this idea even LESS!
Where did "I" *GO*?
I mean, now I'm just
NOWHERE at all!

Hmmmmph!

So if I take away **ME**,
Then I'm NOTHING
and I'm NOWHERE

Well that's not any fun either!

So if being

EVERYTHING

E V E R Y W H E R E

or being

NOTHING

NOWHERE

are both so dull and boring,
then what's my 3RD choice?

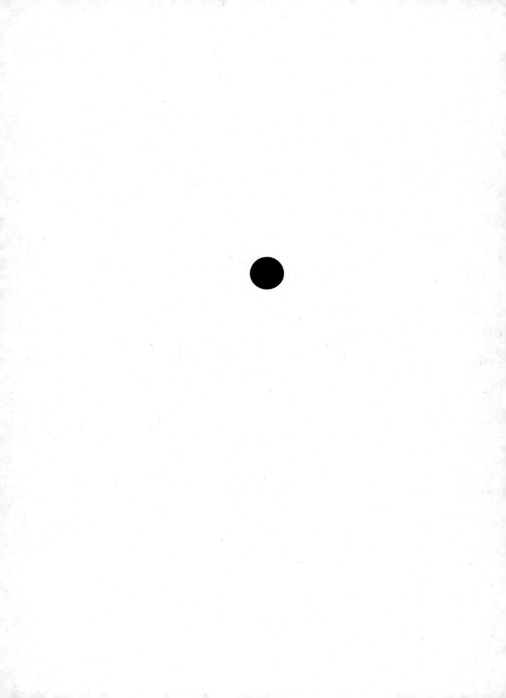

Uh, oh! Back to **ME**
as the **BLACK DOT** again!

OK, so when I pretend that I'm the **BLACK DOT,**

then I'm really pretending that I'm

SOMETHING  SOMEWHERE!

OK, so now I can *GO* over here,

and pretend that I'm not over there!

Or, I can **GO** over here,

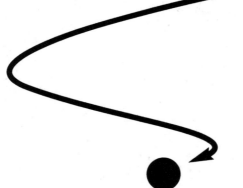

and pretend that
I'm NOT anyplace ELSE!

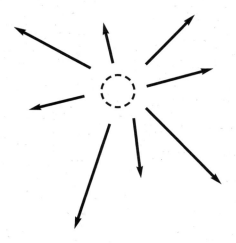

Well, hmmmmm.

Now that I've
m°ved aroUnd a bit,

what else can I do?

?

Well, let's see.
I can change my shape from this

●

into THIS!

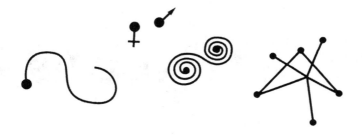

Hey, not too bad.
What else?

Well, I can change my size!
Watch me pretend to

gROW!

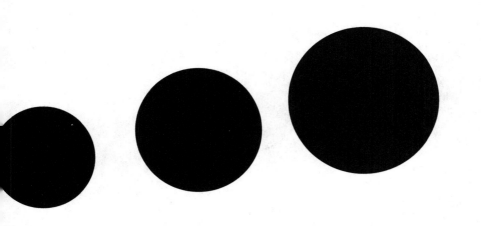

Well, it sure is more FUN
pretending that there's some

NOTHING

to move my

SOMETHING

(the **BLACK DOT**)
around in!

But now that I can change my

S I Z E

and

shape

and even move around a bit,

what else can I do?

?

Well, since I'm already
pretending that I'm

SOMETHING  SOMEWHERE

why don't I also just pretend
that there's something **ELSE**
that's *somewhere* too?

OK, let's try it!

Now here is a picture
of two *somethings*.

WHOOOOOPS!

Now how did I get back to being

EVERYTHING

E V E R Y W H E R E ?

? ? ? ? ?

Oh, I get it!
I forgot to include some

NOTHING

between my two somethings.

#1  #2

There, that's better!

I guess some

NOTHING

is pretty important if there's going
to be some something.

#1 ● #2 ●

(Hmmmmm. Maybe they do
kind of NEED each other!)

Well, since I'm pretending
that I'm two

SOMETHINGS ●
● SOMEWHERE

now I can really begin having

FUN!

#1 ● #2 ●

Now I can come together,

#1 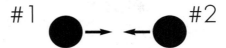 #2

or, at least pretend that I am
coming together.

Or I can pretend that I am
going apart.

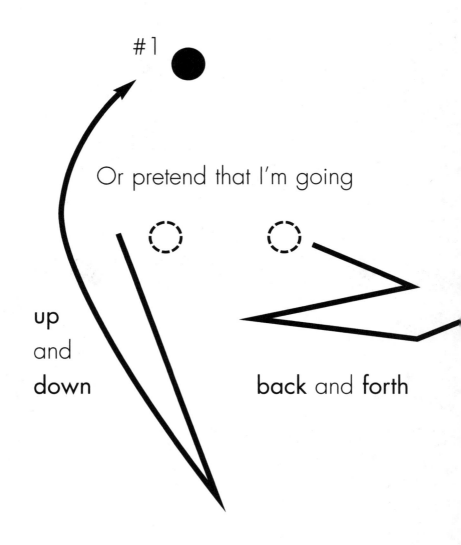

#1

Or pretend that I'm going

up
and
down

back and **forth**

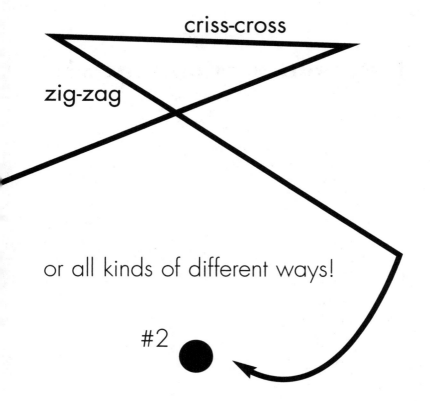

criss-cross

zig-zag

or all kinds of different ways!

#2

But, wait a minute now!

If my #1 **something** goes over here,

#1

I already know that my #2 **something** will go over here!

#1

So where is the **FUN?**

I mean, since I always know exactly
what I'm going to be doing **next**,

there's really nothing, well,

NEW!

I can't surprise myself or
anything simply because
there's really only **ME**

                    p r e t e n d i n g

that I'm these two

SOMETHING S●
● **SOMEWHERE**

Hmmmmm, too bad. It really
seemed like such a good idea, too!

Hey, well what about this!

Since I'm already pretending
that there's **something else**
that's **somewhere,**

why don't I simply pretend that I'm

NOT

p r e t e n d i n g

?

Wow! That's a great idea! By

p r e t e n d i n g

that I'm

<u>NOT</u>

p r e t e n d i n g

that there's **something else,**

it will really *seem* like there
actually *is* **something else**

out there

besides ME!

OK, now how would this work?

Well, in order to

p r e t e n d
that I'm

<u>NOT</u>

p r e t e n d i n g

that there's **something else,**
I can just start pretending that I'm
only **one** of the two black dots.

So now,

what would happen if I started
pretending that I'm *really* **only** my

#1 **BLACK DOT?**

 ?

Well, one thing is for sure!

If I pretended that I'm **only**
my #1 **BLACK DOT,**

then I wouldn't know what
my #2 **BLACK DOT**
would be doing next!

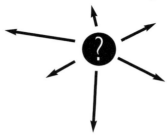

And, if I didn't really know what #2 would be doing NEXT,

then I could be *SURPRISED* and have more

!

OK, so now I'm

p r e t e n d i n g

that my #1 **BLACK DOT**
doesn't know anything
about my #2 **BLACK DOT.**

So, if #1 dot moves over here,

#1

let's see what my #2 dot will do.

#2

#2

Well, look at that!

I would have guessed that my #2 dot would have gone the other way.

#1

Hey, now this could be kind of
EXCITING!

All I have to "do" is to

continue

to **p r e t e n d**

that I'm ONLY my
#1 **BLACK DOT**.

#1 ●

Let's see, now:

"I am only my #1 dot.
I am **NOT** my #2!"

"I am only my #1 dot.
I am **NOT** my #2!"

OK,

I think I've got it straight now.

Hmmmmm.

But suppose I accidentally **remember**
that I'm only just **p r e t e n d i n g**?

Well, that might really spoil my

FUN!

I know!

Just to make really SURE that I can
keep my game going, I'd also
better arrange that I keep

f o r g e t t i n g

that I'm just

p r e t e n d i n g

that I'm only my #1 black dot.

If I continue to forget
that I'm only pretending,
then I can continue to
be S U R P R I S E D !

(Hey, this sure is sounding good!)

But, uh oh!

With only one #2 **BLACK DOT** to have fun with, it'll be much too easy for me to remember again that I'm really pretending to be ONLY my #1 **BLACK DOT**.

What can I do?

I've got it!

I'll just pretend that there's a whole
lot of my #2 dots out there!

And I can always pretend that there's some more, too!

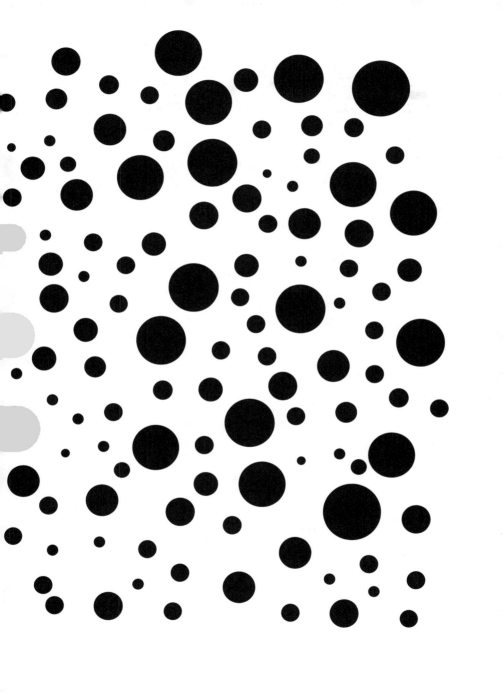

WOW! Look at that!
Think of the possibilities!

With all of those other #2 dots out
there, I won't have any trouble

f o r g e t t i n g

that I'm just

p r e t e n d i n g

that I'm only my #1 black dot.

In fact, after a while,

I might even start really **believing** that my #1 **BLACK DOT** is all that **I am** and all that **I ever have been** and **ever will be.**

 !

And, meanwhile, just look at all
the things that I can pretend to be.

(I wonder what they all mean?)

So now I can play my game by pretending to **b e c o m e** what I'm pretending to **not** be!

All I have to do to get
this **game** started is

to *continue*

to *forget*

that I am only **pretending**
that there's **something else**
out there (⁙) besides **ME.**

Well that seems pretty easy!

OK, let's see now. How should I start my **game**

(And, of course, how should I end it)

?

I mean, I don't want to play the **game** all of the time, you know.

Well, it's probably not
a good idea to start
the **game** with **ME**,

because then I might catch
on too quickly and suddenly
remember that I'm just

pretending it all!

And that would spoil my FUN!

OK, I'd better start the **game** with one of my something elses.

#1  #2

I know!

I'll pretend that I **came**
from one of my #2 dots!

And then I can even
pretend that that #2 dot
had come from another #2!

And on.

And on.

And on.

WOW

!

With all of my #2 dots
tied together like that,

it'll **seem** like my **game** has
already been going on for a long
l o n g time when I start it!

What a clever idea!

OK, to begin my **game**, I'll simply pretend that I suddenly **AM** my #1 dot, and that, somehow, I **came from** one of my #2 dots.

And then, to have some fun, I'll just play with my #2 dots!

And, just for a little change
of pace every now and then,

I think that I'll also arrange
for me to take a lot of

short

little

bre aks

during my **game**.

Hmmmmm.

But how can I keep
on stopping and
starting my **game**
over and over again
without me just catching
on too quickly?

I know!

I'll just pretend that,
every so often, I have to
go to sleep.

(Whatever that is.)

But, of course, when I start my **game** up again, it will have to seem like it had really gone on

WITHOUT **ME**
while I was **sleeping**.

And, when I get really bored and want to end my **game**,

then I'll just

STOP pretending it all

#1

and... drop out!

And I can even make it so that my #2 dots **SEEM** to drop in and out of the **game**, too.

You know, this **game** looks so

EXCITING

that I'm sure I'll want to pretend to be
playing it again and again.

All I have to do is to start pretending
that there's **something else** besides

and the **game** is off
and running again!

Well, it sure beats just
sitting around being

EvERYThiNG

E V E R Y W H E R E

or

NOTHING

NOWHERE

I mean, at least now, something **seems** to be, well,

HAPPENING!

And, if I want to really end my **game**, all I have to do is to

REMEMBER

that I'm only just

PRETENDING

that there's **something else**.

Hmmmmm. But to make sure that I'll be able to remember again who I really am,

I'd better arrange to have some of my #2 dots **remind** me, from time to time, that I'm only just **pretending!**

Oh, I don't think that I'll ever actually forget who I *really* am,

but it sure will be a lot of

FUN

to

p r e t e n d

that I have!

OK, so let the game begin!

WOW!

Just look at this stuff!

By **pretending** to become
what I'm **pretending** to *not* be,
I appear to be

GROWING!

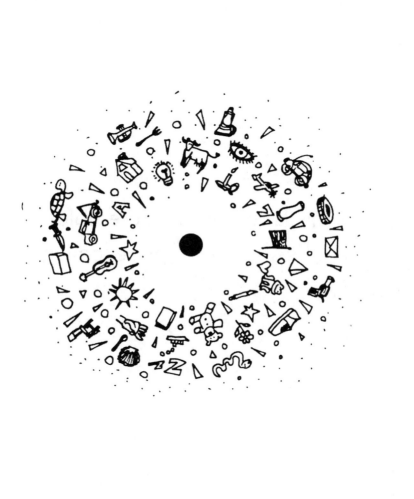

This is absolutely **incredible!**
Just look at what I'm becoming!

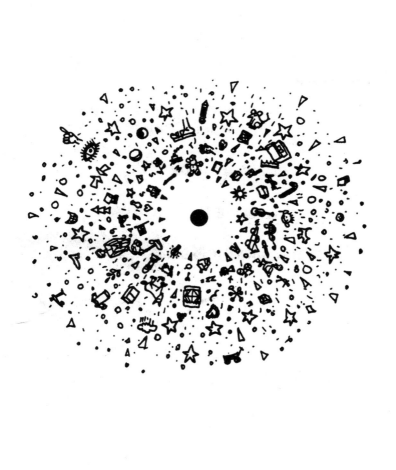

I'm really getting caught up in this whole **game!** I'm wondering if I'm pretending to **become** too MUCH!

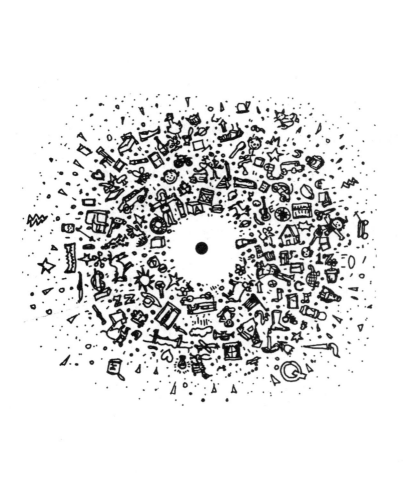

Uh, oh!
Something is happening to me!

I don't seem...
to know...
who...

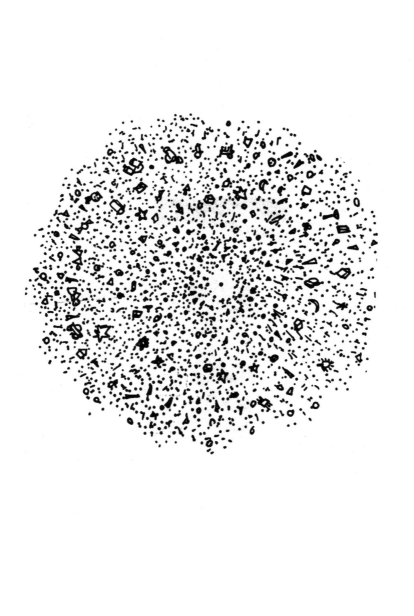

There's something important
that I'm trying to remember!

#1 #2

Do you know what it is?

You know, I think that I'm
so involved in my **game**
that now I've even *forgotten*
that I've **forgotten** that I'm
only **p r e t e n d i n g** that there's
something else besides

What a mess!
Now what do I do?

Oh, well it still is *my* **game,**
and I have to admit that it
sure is **EXCITING!**

I guess that what I'm really forgetting *now* is that, deep down,...

I REALLY DON'T WANT TO END MY GAME!

(Well, not just yet anyway!)

About the Author

Chuck Hillig is the name of one of your #2 dots that you have arranged to remind you, from time to time, that you are really only

PRETENDING IT ALL!

You can contact him through his website, *www.chuckhillig.com*.

Sentient Publications, LLC publishes books on cultural creativity, experimental education, transformative spirituality, holistic health, new science, and ecology, approached from an integral viewpoint. Our authors are intensely interested in exploring the nature of life from fresh perspectives, addressing life's great questions, and fostering the full expression of the human potential. Sentient Publications' books arise from the spirit of inquiry and the richness of the inherent dialogue between writer and reader.

We are very interested in hearing from our readers. To direct suggestions or comments to us, or to be added to our mailing list, please contact:

SENTIENT PUBLICATIONS, LLC
1113 Spruce Street
Boulder, CO 80302
303.443.2188
contact@sentientpublications.com
www.sentientpublications.com